Reset Your Life: Make a New Start

by

Joseph W. Walker III

Reset Your Life Workbook

Contents

Session One: Getting the Most from This Study 5
A Special Introduction by Bishop Joseph W. Walker III

Session Two: The Choice Is Now 9

Session Three: Recognize the Call 15

Session Four: Reassess and Recalibrate 21

Session Five: Reclaim and Rededicate 27

Session Six: Let God Reinvent You and Your World 33

Session Seven: Resurrection: The Great Reset 39

Helps for Group Leaders 45

Notes 48

Session One

Getting the Most from This Study

A Special Introduction by Joseph W. Walker III

What are you facing right now? Take a moment to inventory your life. Be honest. We can't fix what we won't face.

1. Am I happy?

2. How's my physical health?

3. Am I on track to meet my goals?

4. Am I aligned with God's plan for my life?

5. Is my heart in the right place?

6. Are my relationships growing in depth and scope?

7. Am I spending my time wisely?

8. Am I spending enough time in prayer and Bible study?

9. Does my life have purpose and meaning?

10. Am I overcoming my self-defeating behaviors and other obstacles?

This workbook is the companion to *Reset Your Life: Make a New Start.* Like the book, this workbook is designed as a practical guide to a better, more satisfying life – one aligned with biblical principles and God's will. Use this workbook either for private devotion or group study. There is ample space to jot down notes, observations, and questions. You can use this workbook to record your requests and answers to prayer and/or keep a running account of your progress as you enter into the reset process.

Each session of the workbook corresponds to a chapter in *Reset Your Life* and is organized for maximum benefit. Sessions open with a key Scripture passage that sets the stage for the session and compliments the Scriptures quoted in the book. The Scripture is followed by some important points that you won't want to miss and a brief summary of the book chapter. Then there is an opportunity for prayer and sharing joys and concerns followed by an opening prayer. We begin with prayer in order to position ourselves to hear what God will reveal to us through the book, conversation with other Christians, and the Bible.

Now we are ready to begin the reset process, so there are a few warm-up questions to get you thinking and the discussion going. These questions are just to get the conversation off to a good, fun start. Chose the questions that fit your group best. Afterward, we go a little deeper as we rethink the Scripture and reset our lives accordingly. Then, with our minds engaged and our spirits encouraged by God's grace, we are ready to go and live differently. Here you will be asked to write down and commit to doing something you believe God is calling you to do. It can be something as simple as texting a friend or offering yourself in Christian service in the coming week. Finally, each session closes with an affirmation of our reset choices to remind us of God's purpose for us. The session concludes with a prayer to help us redirect our lives in the direction of God's choosing and the Bible's teaching.

It's too easy to be on fire for God. Fires without fuel will just go out quickly and affect nothing. This workbook is designed to take you to the next level in your Christian walk. It is meant to add fuel, so that you can shine your light before all people. I am very excited that you and our church are willing to open ourselves to the great things God is ready to give us. But we must show Him that we are ready to reset our priorities and be His people. Because together with God there is nothing that we cannot do.

Notes, Observations, and Questions

Take as much time as you need and answer the questions below. Make notes and record observations here as needed. We will revisit these questions at the end of the study to see how your answers compare. Be honest. Be open. Be fearless. After answering, share with the group only those things you feel comfortable sharing.

1. Am I happy?

2. How's my physical health?

3. Am I on track to meet my goals?

4. Am I aligned with God's plan for my life?

5. Is my heart in the right place?

6. Are my relationships growing in depth and scope?

7. Am I spending my time wisely?

8. Am I spending enough time in prayer and Bible study?

9. Does my life have purpose and meaning?

10. Am I overcoming my self-defeating behaviors and other obstacles?

Closing Prayer

Dear Heavenly Father, We know that you are a God of Your word and You promise to walk beside us through the valleys of life. And we know that when we can't, when we stumble and fail, You will carry us the rest of the way. Lord, give us the strength to walk in Your ways. Give us the courage to reset our lives, so that we will be pleasing in Your sight. These things we ask in Jesus's name. Amen.

A Special Prayer for You as You Begin This Study

May the Lord bless you and keep you. May the Lord lift up His countenance upon you and give you peace. Holy God, You are our Rock, our Strength, and our Redeemer. You desire that we walk in Your paths. You have given us the Bible for instruction and knowledge of Your perfect will. You have given us each other to support, serve, and love. Grant us the faith, power, and conviction to accomplish what lies before us. World without end. Amen.

—Bishop Joseph W. Walker III

Session Two

Reset: The Choice Is Now

…choose you this day whom ye will serve; whether the gods which your fathers served that were on the other side of the flood, or the gods of the Amorites, in whose land ye dwell; but as for me and my house, we will serve the LORD. And the people answered and said, God forbid that we should forsake the LORD, to serve other gods; For the LORD our God, he it is that brought us up and our fathers out of the land of Egypt, from the house of bondage, and which did those great signs in our sight, and preserved us in all the way wherein we went, and among all the people through whom we passed: And the LORD drove out from before us all the people, even the Amorites which dwelt in the land: therefore will we also serve the LORD; for he is our God.

—Joshua 24: 15-18, KJV

Points to Remember

1. The choice to reset is yours alone. No one can make it for you, and the consequences are never solitary. But your time is not unlimited, so do it now.

2. We love because God loved us first, because love is never defined by the one who is loved. It is defined by the lover.

3. Reset will give you a real relationship with God; and only God can provide your life with purpose.

Summary of Chapter 2 —The Choice Is Now

We all know how indispensable cell phones have become and that sometimes they need a hard reset. So there are also times when we must reset our lives. But unlike a device, even the most advanced, we have a choice whether or not we will recalibrate ourselves so that we can once again, determine the good, acceptable, and perfect will of God. But time is of the essence. Just as Esther was placed in her situation at just the right time to save her people and the prophet Hosea obeyed God in the season of Israel's rebellion, so too must we be ready to receive God's spirit of transformation when He chooses to give it. God is always on time but we must be ready to move when He calls.

Sharing Joys and Concerns

Take a few minutes and share you joys and concerns as you answer these questions:

1. What's going well in your life?
2. Where have you received God's blessing and anointing this week?
3. What's not going well in your life?
4. Who, in particular, needs God's healing, guiding, teaching, motivation, and/or rescue?

Opening Prayer

Dear Holy God, God of power and might. The earth is full of Your glory and we want to give You praise and thanksgiving for all we have and for the good things You desire for us. We know that we make mistakes and need second chances, and we are grateful that You forgive us and that You are there to pick us up when we fall. Be with these people we have mentioned. Bring them the healing they need, and give us the willingness to be Your hands and feet in this world, so that Your kingdom will come on earth as in heaven. We ask these things knowing that You are always on time with Your help for us. In Jesus's name, amen.

Getting Warmed-Up

1. Tell your own cell phone story. What kind of cell do you have? Have you had a similar experience to Bishop Walker's?
2. Are you more like a sprinter or a long-distance runner?
3. Are you more likely to be on time, ten minutes early, late, or are you obviously to the clock?
4. Share a funny story when you were either late or too early and what happened as a result.

Going Deeper: Rethinking the Scripture

1. Take a few minutes and review the story of Esther (pages 17-22). What stands out to you as you read? What commands your attention?

2. Esther 4:14 says, "Yet who knows whether you have come to the kingdom for such a time as this?" Look in your Bible and find who asked Esther that question. What do you think Esther thought when she was asked? Have you ever felt that God placed you in a situation to help someone else? If so, describe the situation.

3. Esther's decision to save her people had far-reaching consequences. Share a time in your life when you made a big decision. What were the intended and unintended consequences?

4. In her actions, we see that Esther was clever as well as courageous. Share a time when you or someone you know acted courageously.

5. Compare and contrast Haman (the villain) and Esther (the heroine). How are they alike? How are the different? Have you met people like Haman? Have you met anyone like Esther? Describe what they are like and how they interacted with you? What role did Mordecai play in the story? Coach? Mentor? Friend? Parent? Counselor? Other? What do you think about Mordecai?

6. Esther's decision long ago has repercussions today, and people still remember and celebrate her bravery. Have someone in the group Google "Purim" to learn more about it. Who are the people in your life that have made decisions that affected you? When you make an important decision do you consider how it will impact other people? Sometimes things aren't black and white and a decision we make might help some people and hurt others. How should we discern what to do when making important decisions? Who do you turn to when you have to make far-reaching decision?

7. Review the story of Hosea (pages 22-35). What speaks to you in the story? What is your first impression of Hosea and Gomer?

8. The story of Hosea and Gomer may seem odd to us. Why would God want Hosea to marry Gomer, who had a long history of unfaithfulness and immorality? What does the relationship between Hosea and Gomer say about our relationship with God?

9. Most people would agree that Hosea got the "short end of the stick" when it came to his relationship with Gomer. But people make bad relationship choices all the time. What should people do when they find themselves in unhealthy relationships?

10. How does the Bible's use Hosea's and Gomer's relationship teach us about God's love for us?

11. Hosea forgave Gomer many times for her infidelity. What is the importance of forgiveness in a relationship? Share a time when you or someone you know offered forgiveness.

12. Some people see God as an old man in the sky who keeps a list of things we do wrong. How do you understand God's forgiveness for you, your friends and family, for your enemies? How might the Lord's Prayer help us understand forgiveness and the need to offer it?

Call to Action: Reset Your Life

Reset is a decision that calls for action. What will do you this week to position yourself to receive God's blessings? What specific things will do you to be a "doer of the Word and not a hearer only"? It can be something as simple as texting a friend to show your concern or offer help. Or there might be a ministry at the church that needs support. Or perhaps your small group might plan to do a service project. List at least two things your will do this week in the space below. You may or may not want to share these with the group, but if you do share them, you have chosen to make yourself accountable to the group and have demonstrated your desire to walk more closely in God's path of right action.

1.

2.

Affirmation (Say this together as a group.)

As I reset my life, I dedicate myself to these choices:

I chose faith over fear.

I chose worship over worry.

I chose love over loneliness.

I chose grace over guilt.

I chose peace over possessions.

I chose praise over pouting.

I chose goodness over gloom.

I chose mercy over misery.

I chose mercy over misery.

I chose salvation over sin.

I chose heaven over hell.

I chose God.

Closing Prayer

Dear Heavenly Father, We ask that You help us as we begin the reset process. When we are weak, give us strength. When we are tempted, give us the power to turn back to You. When we are afraid, give us the love to conquer our fears, because we know: "Perfect love casts out all fear." We are grateful that You will forgive us over and over, and we praise You for Your perfect timing in our lives. Grant us the determination to reset, and thank You for the opportunity. We pray Your blessings on our group and those we have lifted up. Free us for joyful obedience to serve You with a willing heart. In Jesus's name, amen.

Session Three

Recognize the Call

And the angel of the LORD appeared unto him in the flame of fire out of the midst of a bush: and he looked, and, behold, the bush burned with fire, and the bush was not consumed. And Moses said, I will now turn aside, and see this great sight, why the bush is not burnt. And when the LORD saw that he hunted aside to see, God call unto him out of the midst of the bush, and said, Moses, Moses. And he said, Here Am I. And He said, Draw not nigh hither; put off thy shoes from off thy feet, for the place whereon thou standest is holy ground. Moreover he said, I am the God of thy father, the God of Abraham, the God of Isaac, and the God of Jacob. And Moses hid his face, for he was afraid to look upon God. And the LORD said, I have surely seen the affliction of my people which are in Egypt, and have heard their cry by reason of their taskmasters; for I know their sorrows; And I am come down to deliver them out of the hand of the Egyptians, and to bring them up out of that land unto a good land…unto a land flowing with milk and honey…Come now therefore, and I will send thee unto Pharaoh, that thou mayest bring forth my people the children of Israel out of Egypt.

—Genesis 3:2-10, KJV

Points to Remember

1. The good news is that for all its power, for all the hold it has on us, the world is no match for God.

2. God is calling, but it's up to you to "turn aside," investigate, chose, and then act.

3. God has a mission for us, so He will send us opportunities to get back into His will.

Summary of Chapter 3 — Recognize the Call

God's call is an urging of the Spirit. Sometimes the call is gentle; sometimes it's in your face, but it's always saying: "Time to move and claim your destiny. I have a mission and I'm sending you." Mephibosheth and Jonah are two people who reset. Mephibosheth came from a place of barrenness – emptiness, no direction,

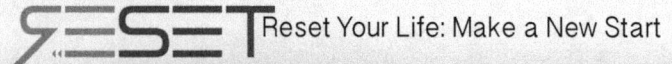

no control, frustration, and fear – when he answered the call to appear before the king and enjoy the bounty of the king's table. Jonah, on the other hand, had everything and nearly threw it all away, because he resisted God's will for his life. God gives us provision for the opportunities He places before us.

Sharing Joys and Concerns

Take a few minutes and share you joys and concerns as you answer to these questions:

1. What's going well in your life?

2. Where have you received God's blessing and anointing this week?

3. What's not going well in your life?

4. Who, in particular, needs God's healing, guiding, teaching, motivation, and/or rescue?

Opening Prayer

Dear Lord, We praise You like the saints of old: holy, holy, holy are You. You are the source of all that we are and ever hope to be. You are the sovereign king of the universe and beyond. Thank you for loving us enough to give each one of us a destiny with purpose and meaning. We know that not only have You prepared for us a feast at Your heavenly table, but You are with us here and now, in this very room. We ask Your healing, guidance, support, and sustaining hand to be upon us and those we have lifted up. We pray for opportunities to show You how much we are willing to do for the sake of bringing Your kingdom on earth as it is in heaven. In Jesus's name, amen.

Getting Warmed-Up

1. Are you a summer, fall, winter, or spring sort of person?

2. Would you rather watch from the stands, coach from the sidelines, or be out on the field playing?

3. Do you prefer partying with a large group of people or spending a quiet evening with just a few friends?

4. What did you want to be when you grew up when you were five or six?

Going Deeper: Rethinking the Scripture

1. Reread and review the story of Mephibosheth on pages 41-56 in the book. Mephibosheth was the son of Jonathan and grandson of Israel's King Saul. The boy was five years old when his father and grandfather were killed in battle with the Philistines at Mt. Gilboa near the Jezreel Valley. Learning of his son's death, Saul took his own life. It was also customary at that time that when a ruler was defeated, his family would be killed as well so that there would be no lineage of that ruler left to reclaim the throne. This held true for Saul's other sons and grandsons. However, according to 2 Samuel 4:4, we learn that Mephibosheth survived but that he was lame in both feet due to an accident. His nurse while fleeing the conquering army picked him up and fled, but somehow in her haste, the boy fell and became crippled as a result. Whether or not, a crippled person could even be king in those ancient times is an open question, but at the very least, Mephibosheth felt the curse of his family's defeat.

2. What purpose might Mephibosheth have played in King David's reign? Do you believe that David was acting with pure intentions for the sake of his dead friend, Jonathan, or you think that there might have been some self-interest in his kindness toward Mephibosheth? What other reasons might King David have had for his kindness toward Mephibosheth?

3. Share a time in your life when you felt boxed in by someone or something. Perhaps this was a teacher, coach, co-worker, boss, friend, family member, significant other, or yourself. How did it feel and what did/do you do about it?

4. "Lo Debar" (page 42) means "no pasture" or "no word." It is a desolate, barren place, and it describes what some people experience in their day-to-day living—emptiness, lack of direction, lack of control, frustration, and/or fear. Have you or someone you know ever struggles with these obstacles? Share a time when you were lonely and what you did about it.

5. Lo Debar is also a place of isolation. When people are hurting, they often turn inward and a kind of negative introspection can cause them to spiral further downward, making it hard to receive help from someone else. What are some helpful ways to approach and offer help, comfort, and encourage to someone who is hurting, either physically, emotionally, or spiritually?

6. When someone is hurting what are some things that you should never say to a person?

7. David might have been an unlikely source of help for Mephibosheth, but through David, God took care of him. Share a time when you received help from an unexpected source or person.

8. On page 49, Bishop Walker says that "God promises that in due season, you're going to reap, but if you faint now, you won't see the breakthrough." How can we keep going when we want to give up? How can the church be a resource for encouragement?

9. Despite Saul's enemies, his family line did continue through Mephibosheth's son Micha, also spelled Mica or Micah. See 2 Samuel 9:12 and 1 Chronicles 9:39-44. Saul's royal bloodline continued. You also have royal blood because you are a child of God, our king. How might knowing that someone has royal blood affect how you treat them? Why are we prone to treat the rich differently from the poor?

10. Review the story of Jonah on pages 55-58. Who was Jonah and why did he run away from God's call? God doesn't call us to easy. He calls us to hard. What are there some ways that we might sympathize with Jonah?

11. Jonah was not keen to help his enemies. But as Christians we are called to love our enemies. Matthew 5:44 says, "But I say unto you, Love your enemies, bless them that curse you, do good to them that hate you, and pray for them which despitefully use you, and persecute you." Share a time when you or someone you know was persecuted. Share a time when an enemy became a friend or when you did what the Bible says and blessed the person who cursed you.

12. Read Jonah 1:6-15 and recall how Jonah ended up in the belly of that great fish and how he repented, 2:9. In your experience, do people change for the better only when they have no other choice? What motivates people to change or reset? In your experience, what works best incentives or threats, the carrot or stick? Might there be an appropriate time for each?

13. The Bible gives a graphic picture of the fish vomiting Jonah out (Jonah 2:10). Jonah must have been a terrible mess, but God still wanted him for the mission. Share a time when you found yourself in a mess and what happened after that.

14. Share a time in your life or someone you know when God took something bad that had happened can used it for good.

Call to Action: Reset Your Life

Reset is a decision that calls for action. What will do you this week to position yourself to receive God's blessings? List at least two things your will do this week in the space below. You may or may not want to share these with the group, but if you do share them, you have chosen to make yourself accountable to the group and have demonstrated your desire to walk more closely in God's path of right action.

1.

2.

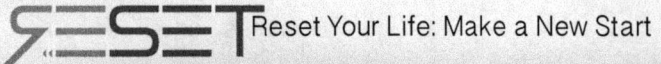

Affirmation (Say this together as a group.)

As I continue to reset my life, I promise that this week:

I will not let distractions get in the way of my walk with God;

I will do my best to heed God's call;

I will be kind to my enemies;

I will reach out to hurting people with God's mercy and goodness to the best of my ability.

I will make God proud to be my Father.

Closing Prayer

Dear God, Thank you for coming to us in our places of barrenness. Thank You for Your steadfast faithfulness in loving us no matter what we've done or how far we've wondered. Equip us to share Your grace with others who are hurting and in need of a kind word. Equip us to take a stand for You in this world, so that You will be proud of us, Your children. Your heirs. In Jesus's name, amen.

Session Four

Reassess and Recalibrate

And as he [Saul] journeyed, he came near Damascus: and suddenly there shined round about him a light from heaven: And he fell to the earth, and heard a voice saying unto him, Saul, Saul, why persecutest thou me? And he said, Who art thou, Lord? And the Lord said, I am Jesus whom thou persecutest: it is hard for thee to kick against the pricks. And he trembling and astonished said, Lord, what wilt thou have me to do? And the Lord said unto him, Arise, and go into the city, and it shall be told thee what thou must do.

—Acts 9:3-6, KJV

Points to Remember

1. God speaks to us through the Bible, reason, experience, and tradition and also through the actions of other faithful Christians.

2. Following Jesus Christ is the only way we find complete and meaningful happiness, fulfillment, and purpose in life.

3. Even the most violent enemy of God can become His truest advocate and champion.

Summary of Chapter 4 — Reassess and Recalibrate

Before the Apostle Paul became a church planter, author of many letters that we have preserved for us in the Bible, and one of the greatest proponents of Jesus Christ in history, he was simply known as Saul of Tarsus: murderer, business man, and student. But God chose Saul and gave him a new name, Paul, signifying his new relationship with Him. Jacob was a liar, cheat, and schemer until he had a powerful encounter with God, who changed his name to Israel, signifying his new mission and purpose. Paul's and Israel's new names also cemented their commitment to God. When we allow God to meet us where we are, we can become followers of Jesus; and as a result, we take His name and become a Christian. Our new name signifies our commitment to

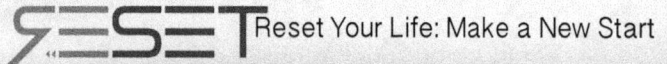

living a Godly life and promising to return to God when we stray away from Him. And by giving us the name Christian, and adopting us as His child, God promises to ever-graciously receive us and forgive our sin.

Sharing Joys and Concerns

Take a few minutes and share you joys and concerns as you answer to these questions:

1. What's going well in your life?

2. Where have you received God's blessing and anointing this week?

3. What's not going well in your life?

4. Who, in particular, needs God's healing, guiding, teaching, motivation, and/or rescue?

Opening Prayer

Dear Father, There are things we need to leave behind so that we may be better followers of You. Relieve us of our failure, discontent, hate, pride, and the unneeded baggage of bad relationships. Bless these people and situations we have mentioned. Let them know that You are present, ready, and able to care for them in their time of need. And let us be Your faithful witnesses as we strive together to make this world a better place.

Getting Warmed-Up

1. Are you a cat, dog, fish, or plant person?

2. What's your favorite way to spend a quiet afternoon?

3. Would you rather camp out in the wilderness or rest in the comfort of a luxury hotel?

4. Who is someone who has mentored you?

Going Deeper: Rethinking the Scripture

1. Paul was not accepted easily by Jesus's followers after he reset. Why do you think that was? Share a time when you or someone you know turned over a new leaf and how people responded.

2. On page 63, Bishop Walker says, "You too are a chosen instrument of God! Your mission is uniquely

yours, and it is every bit as real as Saul's." How do you feel about that? Does it make you feel special, excited, nervous, anxious, fearful, something else?

3. Share with the group how your reset is going. Are you receiving the support you need? Has your reset created a new thirst or curiosity for studying the Bible? Are you becoming more aware of the people and their needs around you? Are you resisting the change or are you embracing it whole heartedly? Paul probably shared some of your thoughts and feelings.

4. Why is Ananias important to Paul's reset? Ananias had a mission too—to facilitate Paul's reset. When was a time when someone was an Ananias to you or when you acted as Ananias for someone else?

5. God may give us one just one mission but many. Have you ever taken on a mission from God and run with it? What were the results? What did you learn? Would you do anything differently this time?

6. Acquaint or reacquaint yourself with the story of Jacob. Who was he? Who were his parents? Who was his twin brother and what was their relationship? What was his family like? Do you know of people in your life who are similar to Jacob, that is, they can't really be trusted? How would be respond if you met Jacob at work, at a party, at a family gathering?

7. Jacob is the best trickster he knew until he met his future father-in-law, Laban. Read Genesis 29:18-25 to see what kind of person Laban was. Put yourself in Jacob's place, what would you have done? Put yourself in Rebekah and Leah's place, how would you have felt? What would you have done?

8. Genesis 32:24 says that "And Jacob was left alone." Why was Jacob alone and what was he doing there?

9. Jacob wrestled with an angel "until the breaking of the day" (Genesis 32:24). The record of this incident is one of the most difficult passages of the Bible to translate because it is not clear who the person is who Jacob wrestles. The text doesn't want to say that Jacob fought with God directly, but when Jacob names the place Peniel, which means: "I have seen God fact to face, and my life is preserved" (Genesis 32:30), there is an indication that, at least, Jacob thought he was wrestling with God.

10. Jacob is injured by his forceful encounter with God. His hip is disjointed. What does this say about their wrestling? But it also appears that, at one point, Jacob gains the upper hand and threatens not to let go until the angel blesses him. The angel does so by changing Jacob's name to Israel. While the meaning of "Israel"

is unclear, among the possibilities are: "power with God," "God rules," "prince of God," "triumphant with God", "who prevails with God," "God fights/struggles," and "he who struggles with God."

11. On page 68, Bishop Walker says that God "authorizes spiritual U-turns." Discuss what it means to make a spiritual U-turn. Paul's and Israel's were dramatic turn-abouts, but many times, all we need to do is make small course corrections. What are some things that help people make changes in their life for the better?

12. God made commitments and promises to Israel. God promised land, blessing, protection, provision, and presence. What do these things have in common? What does God promise us? you?

13. Jacob/Israel makes a three-fold promise back to God: that God would be his God wherever he goes; that he will set up a memorial to commemorate the event; and that whatever blessing he receives, he will give a tenth, a tithe, back to God. What promises have you made to God in terms of your time, presence, gifts, service, and witness to Him?

Call to Action: Reset Your Life

Reset is a decision that calls for action. What will do you this week to position yourself to receive God's blessings? List at least two things you will do this week in the space below. You may or may not want to share these with the group, but if you do share them, you have chosen to make yourself accountable to the group and have demonstrated your desire to walk more closely in God's path of right action.

1.

2.

Affirmation (Say this together as a group.)

    Lord, we are getting away from low-down people.

    We are tired of people who don't want anything and don't want anybody else to have anything.

    Lord, lift us up. Let us stand. Let us stand together.

    Plant our feet on high ground.

Closing Prayer

    Dear Lord, Help us to stop struggling and accept Your will for our lives. Because we know that when You fully accept You, You will not leave us where we are or abandon us to the past. You are the God of moving into the future. The desire of Your heart is to bless us and for us to bless others through the grace, love, and mercy that You have shown us. For these things we thank You. Be with us as we reset this week. Help us return to You. Help us to reassess and recalibrate our goals and behavior. Help us reflect Your glory for the world to see, so that others may know the joy of Your salvation. In Jesus's name, amen.

Session Five

Reclaim and Rededicate

O LORD, thou hast searched me, and known me.

Thou knowest my downsitting and mine uprising, thou understandest my thought afar off.

Thou compassest my path and my lying down, and art acquainted with all my ways.

For there is not a word in my tongue, but, lo, O LORD, thou knowest it altogether.

Thou hast beset me behind and before, and laid thine hand upon me.

Such knowledge is too wonderful for me; it is high, I cannot attain unto it.

Whither shall I go from thy spirit? or whither shall I flee from thy presence?

If I ascend up into heaven, thou art there: if I make my bed in hell, behold, thou art there.

If I take the wings of the morning, and dwell in the uttermost parts of the sea;

Even there shall thy hand lead me, and thy right hand shall hold me.

If I say, Surely the darkness shall cover me; even the night shall be light about me.

Yea, the darkness hideth not from thee; but the night shineth as the day: the darkness and the light are both alike to thee.

For thou hast possessed my reins: thou hast covered me in my mother's womb.

I will praise thee; for I am fearfully and wonderfully made: marvellous are thy works; and that my soul knoweth right well.

My substance was not hid from thee, when I was made in secret, and curiously wrought in the lowest parts of the earth.

Thine eyes did see my substance, yet being unperfect; and in thy book all my members were written, which in continuance were fashioned, when as yet there was none of them.

How precious also are thy thoughts unto me, O God! how great is the sum of them!

If I should count them, they are more in number than the sand: when I awake, I am still with thee.

Surely thou wilt slay the wicked, O God: depart from me therefore, ye bloody men.

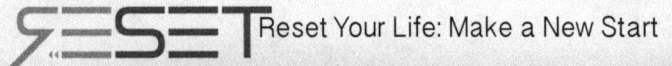

For they speak against thee wickedly, and thine enemies take thy name in vain.

Do not I hate them, O LORD, that hate thee? and am not I grieved with those that rise up against thee?

I hate them with perfect hatred: I count them mine enemies.

Search me, O God, and know my heart: try me, and know my thoughts:

And see if there be any wicked way in me, and lead me in the way everlasting.

— Psalm 139, KJV

Points to Remember

1. There can be no purification without separation. Our hearts cannot be clean unless we create distance between ourselves and what was.

2. God expects conviction from us, so we must be willing to sacrifice those things that are not of God and put away false idols.

3. God is the best thing that can or could happen to us. Let's get excited and tell somebody.

Summary of Chapter 5 — Reclaim and Rededicate

To reclaim the destiny and purpose God wants to give, we must first separate ourselves from the people, places, and things that tempt us to stray away from God. God cannot "create in us a clean heart" until we break away from those idols that distract and threaten our well-being. The stories of Jacob and Joshua offer us key lessons on how to reset. First, we must put the past behind us. Second, we must symbolize our willingness to sacrifice. It is helpful to have a tangible reminder, an altar that can serve to call us back to God. Third, we must realize that to get back our fire for God, we may need to let some things die in our lives, so that we can truly live. But we are often caught between two realities: God's and the world's. It can be hard to let go, but God expects our commitment and conviction to try. And with His help, we will succeed. Fourth, we must realize that we aren't in this alone. God has given us the community of faithful believers, the Church, to strengthen our resolve, teach us His ways, and hold us accountable for our rededication.

Sharing Joys and Concerns

Take a few minutes and share you joys and concerns as you answer to these questions:

1. What's going well in your life?

2. Where have you received God's blessing and anointing this week?

3. What's not going well in your life?

4. Who, in particular, needs God's healing, guiding, teaching, motivation, and/or rescue?

Opening Prayer

Dear Holy God, You know our innermost being. You know us by name and the number of hairs on our head. O God, search me and try me. Cleanse me of any wickedness, hateful, and selfish pride. Lead me in the way to everlasting life. And we ask Your kindness and mercy on these people and situations we have mentioned. We pray for Your healing touch. We pray that they will know the fullness of life. And if they are too weak, give them the strength to confront and defeat their demons. And Lord, help us to be an encourager, a giver, and a healer in our relationships as well. In Jesus's name, amen.

Getting Warmed-Up

1. When you can, do you like to take afternoon naps?

2. Briefly describe your first car and who taught you to drive.

3. If your house was on fire, assuming that all the people and pets are safe, what are three things that you'd try to save?

Going Deeper: Rethinking the Scripture

1. On page 85, Bishop Walker says that there can be no separation from the things that hold us down and back without some agitation. "Sin has attached itself to you the way dirt and grim attach themselves to

your clothes." To get clean, we need a good scrubbing, not with soap but with the power of the Holy Spirit. What are some ways that God gives people a "good scrubbing"? What are some ways that God has disrupted your life?

2. One of the warm-up questions asks if the house was on fire and you knew that all the people and pets were safe, what three things are important enough for you to run back into the house to save? Share with the group your three things and why they are so important.

3. Idols are things that get in the way in our relationship with God. Idols can also be priorities that we put ahead of our relationship with God. Take a minute and list a couple of your priorities. What are the church's priorities? What are God's priorities? Where do your priorities line up with the church's and God's? Where do they diverge?

4. It took Jacob a long time to change his deceitful ways. In your opinion, why does it take so long for people to do the things they should? Why are people so reluctant to give up on bad relationships?

5. God wants us to connect with Him and keep that connection free from interference. On a scale of one to ten (one being low and ten being high), how is your relationship with God today?

6. Here are ways we can connect with God: prayer, Bible study, worship, Christian service, unselfish giving, and gracious hospitality. Which are easiest for you? Which are hardest?

How would your life be different if you prioritized these things?

7. Jesus tells us in Matthew 6:24 (See page 102.): "No one can serve two masters; for either he will have the one and love the others, or else he will be loyal to the one and despise the others. You cannot serve God and mammon." Do you know people (without giving names or being judgmental) who overvalue their car? Do you? Do you know people who worship their job over their family? Do you? Or who want status more than a relationship with God? Do you? How could their lives be better if they gave higher priority to God?

8. Joshua (page 103) offers himself and his family as a paradigm: "But as for me and my house, we will serve the Lord" (Joshua 24:15). In your household how do you serve God? Do you pray at meals? Do you have family devotions? Do you pray with your children and spouse daily? How might your family be different if you made your relationship with God more visible at home?

9. Share a time in your life when you felt close to God.

10. We all are aware of the glitter and gold the world offers and we are drawn to it like moths to a flame. What things does a relationship with God offer us?

11. Tell a time when you shared some exciting news. How did it feel? What was the response?

12. If we believe that God is the best thing that ever happened to us, why do some of us have such a difficult time sharing about it? If you have a hard time talking about your relationship with God to friends, why not just invite them to church and they can experience it for themselves?

Call to Action: Reset Your Life

Reset is a decision that calls for action. What will do you this week to position yourself to receive God's blessings? List at least two things your will do this week in the space below. You may or may not want to share these with the group, but if you do share them, you have chosen to make yourself accountable to the group and have demonstrated your desire to walk more closely in God's path of right action.

1.

2.

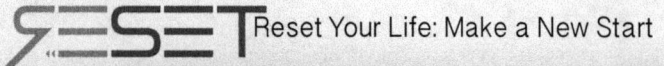

Affirmation (Say this together as a group.)

Nothing can separate us from the love of God.

I will give God and my relationship with His priority this week.

I promise to meditate on where the Lord found me and where he might take me.

Closing Prayer

Dear Lord, We confess that we need to make our relationship with You a higher priority. Grant us the conviction to pray more often, give of ourselves more freely, and meditate on Your Word daily. Help us to move forward from here and leave the hurtful, unhelpful, and unhealthy past behind. Guide us to rededicate our lives to You and Your service. Help us be doers of the word and not hearers only. Protect and defend us, because as for us and our house, we will serve the Lord. In Jesus's name, amen.

Session Six

Let God Reinvent You and Your World

And I saw a new heaven and a new earth: for the first heaven and the first earth were passed away; and there was no more sea. And I John saw the holy city, new Jerusalem, coming down from God out of heaven, prepared as a bride adorned for her husband. And I heard a great voice out of heaven saying, Behold, the tabernacle of God is with men, and he will dwell with them, and they shall be his people, and God himself shall be with them, and be their God. And God shall wipe away all tears from their eyes; and there shall be no more death, neither sorrow, nor crying, neither shall there be any more pain: for the former things are passed away. And he that sat upon the throne said, Behold, I make all things new. And he said unto me, Write: for these words are true and faithful. And he said unto me, It is done. I am Alpha and Omega, the beginning and the end. I will give unto him that is athirst of the fountain of the water of life freely.

—Revelation 21:1-6, KJV

Points to Remember

1. To answer God's call to reset, we must embrace our role as a visionary, dreamer, and destiny chases whether or not others understand or support us.

2. God wants us to move forward and the world we enter once we reset is filled with hope and promise.

3. When we "get out of our boat," even if we start to sink, God will grab us and never let us go.

4. When God reinvents us, we become known as people of transformation, love, and service.

Summary of Chapter 6 — Let God Reinvent You and Your World

We may have issues and a complicated past, but all of us have the ability to discern God's call. And God won't stop calling our name until we answer "Yes, Lord, send me." This chapter describes three people: Noah, Peter, and Mary Magdalene. God reinvented each of them and their world and the legacies of their lives still benefit us today. Noah, obeyed God and through him and his family, God started over with a world that could be redeemed. Peter was impetuous and stubborn, but when reset these some traits helped Peter hold fast to Jesus and become a dependable rock on which the church was later built. When God reinvented Mary Magdalene, she was freed of her demons and become the first witness to Jesus's resurrection. In addition she assumed a leadership role in the young church. All things that would have been impossible before.

Sharing Joys and Concerns

Take a few minutes and share you joys and concerns as you answer to these questions:

1. What's going well in your life?

2. Where have you received God's blessing and anointing this week?

3. What's not going well in your life?

4. Who, in particular, needs God's healing, guiding, teaching, motivation, and/or rescue?

Opening Prayer

Dear Lord Jesus, Be our guest and let each one here be blessed. We are grateful for Your presence here among us. We are truly grateful for Your call to reset our lives, but we know that we cannot reinvent ourselves. Only You can reinvent us and set us on a path that will reinvent the world with justice, mercy, steadfast loving kindness. Be with those we have mentioned, those who are on our hearts today, those who need Your healing and saving touch. We know that You call us by name and will never give up on us. Help us to share that good news in our world and be instruments of Your peace. In Jesus's name, amen.

Getting Warmed-Up

1. Do you think before you talk or do you talk as you think?

2. Do you make decisions fast or do you mull over the facts before you act?

3. What kind of music do you listen to? What's the name of a song you know all the lyrics to?

Going Deeper: Rethinking the Scripture

1. Share a time when you felt close to God this week?

2. We live in evil times not unlike Noah, but somehow Noah remained faithful to God. What are some ways we can remain faithful to God in the midst of our conflicting priorities, uncertain circumstances, and/or poor choices?

3. God reset the world with a faithful remnant, Noah and his family, rather than destroy it completely. What does this say to you about who God is?

4. Noah was skilled in harvesting crops, what might he have thought when God gave him a task to build the ark, which was probably completely outside of his skill set? What would you think if God asked you to retool and revise your life for his mission even if it meant saving the world?

5. When God resets you, he takes the good you already have and multiplies it, but sometimes the reset doesn't last and we have to repent and reset again. Read Genesis 9:20-25 to see "the rest of the story." Clearly neither Noah nor his family is perfect. Describe what happened in Noah's dysfunctional family after the Flood.

6. Reread Matthew 14:22-32 on pages 112-113. Retell the story in your own words. If you had to write a headline for that story, what would it be?

7. What kind of man was Peter? Do you know people like him? How are you like and unlike him?

8. Jesus knew Peter was special and had strong leadership abilities; yet, Jesus also knew that Peter was flawed. Like us, Peter was a mixture of strength and weakness. But one thing that made Peter a "rock" was his tenacity and desire to be key to God's mission. List some of your strengths. (NOTE: If appropriate, let the group tell each person a strength that they see in that person. This requires that members have a high level of trust and faith in the group. It also takes a group that knows each other well, so if you or your group is not ready for this, save it for another time.)

9. On pages 117-118, Bishop Walker says that some of our "ships," whether friend*ships*, partner*ships*, or relation*ships*, are too small to get us where God is taking us. Are there "ships" in your life that you need to let go? Share a time when you had to let go of something that was important to you. It might be a relationship, but it might also be an object, memory, ambition, grudge, job, or something else.

10. Peter has the courage to step out of the boat. What does it take for a person to step out and/or step up? Share a time when someone's encouragement made a big difference in your life, or share a time when you encouraged someone.

11. As also know that when Peter stepped out of the boat, he did walk on water to Jesus. But as soon as he took his eyes off Jesus, he began to sink. How do you think Peter felt? What do you think the other disciples still in the boat thought?

12. Bishop Walker reminds us that it takes time with Jesus to be able to "walk on water," i.e., do what is impossible. But Jesus calls his disciples, us, to do just that. It's not up to us to say whether or not something is impossible. Our task is to spend time with the Master and be ready when He calls. Your situation may not change, but you will. What are there seemingly impossible situations in your life right now?

13. God wants us to keep our eyes on Him, our destination and not our situation. (See pages 122-123.) Why should we not define someone by their failures? (See pages 124-125.)

14. Jesus healed Mary Magdalene and she became a follower of Jesus. She was an unlikely witness to Jesus's resurrection, so much so that when she told the disciples, they didn't believe her. Who are the people in your life who can support your reset?

15. Mary Magdalene lived a life of transformation, love, and service. In what ways do you think she changed? How do you think her former friends and family saw her when she was reinvented by Jesus? Who are the people and situations that need your transformation, love, and service?

Call to Action: Reset Your Life

Reset is a decision that calls for action. What will do you this week to position yourself to receive God's blessings? List at least two things your will do this week in the space below. You may or may not want to share these with the group, but if you do share them, you have chosen to make yourself accountable to the group and have demonstrated your desire to walk more closely in God's path of right action.

1.

2.

Affirmation (Say this together as a group.)

To be reset means that we hand our lives over to God.

To be reset means that we are the clay and God is the potter.

To be reset means being willing to do whatever it takes.

To be reset means to have clear purpose, a healthy sense of pride, and a strong character.

To be reset means that the mess I've made of my life can be reinvented as something new that conforms to God's will for me.

Lord, help us commit to allowing God to reinvent us this week.

Closing Prayer

Dear God, You are the master potter, the Great Physician, the Good Shepherd, and our loving Father. We praise You for Your willingness to hold on to us when we fall, reach out for us when we stumble, and hold us up when we are sinking under the weight of our sin and others' sin toward us. We pray for Your help this week as well as our commitment to get out of our boats and keep walking toward You. In Jesus's name, amen.

Session Seven

Resurrection: The Great Reset

Jesus said unto her, I am the resurrection, and the life: he that believeth in me, though he were dead, yet shall he live: And whosoever liveth and believeth in me shall never die. Believest thou this? She saith unto him, Yea, Lord: I believe that thou art the Christ, the Son of God, which should come into the world.

—John 11:25-27

Points to Remember

1. The resurrection of Jesus makes our reset and all other resets possible. There was no bigger moment in history.

2. The best leaders are those who serve others unselfishly. They are servant-leaders who strive to follow the example of Jesus. Servant-leaders walk beside others where the road is rocky and steep.

3. Because Jesus took on our humanity, we can take on his divinity.

4. The church is a Resurrection People. You never have to go it alone.

Summary of Chapter 7 — Resurrection: The Great Reset

Jesus is the only way, and it is through the power of God that we can share in the power of the resurrection. Jesus was fully human and fully divine. And those who have faith in Him can sum it up in three simple statements: Christ has died. Christ has risen. Christ will come again. These facts encompass the mystery of faith and remind us that nothing can separate us from the love of God. Nothing. But no one is totally immune to desires of the flesh, so we must surrender to God, our Father, who then makes us His children, so that we can enter into the joy of salvation and feast at His heavenly banquet. Jesus was more than a good, moral person who we need to emulate. In fact, if we try, we will fail. He is the One and Only. We can't be Him, because he was God's perfect Son. But because He was human, He knows our struggles, pain, and temptations. The difference

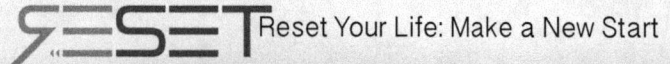

between what Jesus does for us and what the gods of all other religions does for their followers is this: our God suffered, died and rose for us. God does not require us to die for Him. God wants us to live for Him and serve Him as He transforms us and our world. Only God has the power to resurrect our lives, our world, our future. All we have to do is accept His love and say, "OK, God. I'm here. Send me."

Sharing Joys and Concerns

Take a few minutes and share you joys and concerns as you answer to these questions:

1. What's going well in your life?
2. Where have you received God's blessing and anointing this week?
3. What's not going well in your life?
4. Who, in particular, needs God's healing, guiding, teaching, motivation, and/or rescue?

Opening Prayer

Dear God, as this study comes to a close, we pray for a resurrection in our lives. We know that all power in heaven and earth are Yours. We know You are ready and able to turn our mourning into dancing, our grief into joy, our anger into mercy, and our sickness into victory. We also know that as long as we are in this world, there will be suffering and death. But we look beyond our here and now, and celebrate the future You have for us. Help us to keep this perspective when we face trials and tribulations. Sometimes we just forget. Help those we've lifted up, know the comfort and assurance only You can give. Heal those who need You touch, and let us show the world that we are a Resurrection People and walk in Your ways.

Getting Warmed-Up

1. What is your favorite reality TV show?

2. Would you rather fly to the moon, vacation on the French Riviera, shop till you drop, or have a gourmet meal at a five-star restaurant?

3. If you could choose to change one thing about yourself, what would it be?

Going Deeper: Rethinking the Scripture

1. Share how God was real to you this week.

2. Share a time where you knew that God was speaking to you but you didn't answer or didn't answer as well as you should have or maybe wanted to.

3. Jesus was God in the flesh. He was God with us. If you met Jesus on the street, what do you think he'd be like?

4. Why is it so hard to some people to serve others? What is the difference between caring for someone and taking care of someone?

5. Name some people who you consider to be strong leaders. They might be people you know personally or people you've only heard about.

6. What qualities do you look for in a person you are willing to follow?

7. Read the story of the prodigal son. You can find it in Luke 15:11-32. With which character do you most readily identify: the prodigal son, the father, the elder brother? Why?

8. On page 152, Bishop Walker says: "The story of the prodigal son also answers the question of why God sometimes lets us fall so far….God allows those things so that when he is there to rescue you, to reset you, no one else gets the glory." What are your thoughts? Do you agree with Bishop Walker?

9. Jesus is our savior for a reason. Review pages 152-153 and list as many reasons as you can.

10. If you had to summarize the Good News for someone who had never heard of it and that person wanted to learn more, what would you say? How would you begin?

11. When Bishop Walker says (page 157) that Jesus tool on our humanity, so that we could take on his divinity. What does that mean to you?

12. The church is called to be a resurrection people. How can the church do a better job fulfilling its call? What are some ways that you and/or your group might help?

13. Share what you have learned from this study. Was it worth your time and energy? Are there things that you will do differently? Do you believe that your reset was successfully launched? What would you like to study next?

14. What new dreams do you have for God's kingdom? What new places is God calling you to go? Are you ready to step forward, get out of the boat, and follow through with your reset?

Call to Action: Reset Your Life

Reset is a decision that calls for action. List some ways you can celebrate your reset. You might want to celebrate as a group as well. Then write down two things you will do this week to honor God by your service to others.

Ways to celebrate:

1.

2.

Ways to serve others this week:

1.

2.

To check your reset progress from the first session, please answer these questions again and compare with the answers you made at the beginning of the study.

1. Am I happy?

2. How's my physical health?

3. Am I on track to meet my goals?

4. Am I aligned with God's plan for my life?

5. Is my heart in the right place?

6. Are my relationships growing in depth and scope?

7. Am I spending my time wisely?

8. Am I spending enough time in prayer and Bible study?

9. Does my life have purpose and meaning?

10. Am I overcoming my self-defeating behaviors and other obstacles?

Affirmation (Say this together as a group.)

We are God's Resurrection People:

    We are hopeful.

    We are not apologetic.

    We are not afraid.

    We are resolute.

    We are focused.

    We are kind.

    We are strong.

    We have purpose.

Closing Prayer

Dear Lord and Savior, You have the power to make all things new. You have the power to resurrect us from our ashes and set us working for Your glory. We confess that we've only just begun, but we are not afraid and we are eager to move forward. Thank You for this study and what we have learned. Thank You for our leadership and all they do to serve us. Bless us as we walk with confidence into a bright future, because with You nothing is impossible. You are our God and we are Your people. Glory to God. Amen.

Helps for Group Leaders

As a group leader, your role is to facilitate the sessions using this workbook and the book, *Reset Your Life: Make a New Start* by Bishop Joseph W. Walker, III. You might find some newsprint, or a chalkboard helpful to write down prayer requests or questions as they arise in group conversation.

Helpful Hints

Read the corresponding chapter in *Reset Your Life: Make a New Start* before the group session. Make note of the scripture references prior to the session. Study the Scripture and refer to more than one translation if that is helpful to you. What speaks to you personally? What do you think God is trying to communicate to you?

- Look ahead and select specific discussion questions you plan to cover. Please don't feel compelled to answer every question. Chose the questions that best suit your group.

- Be the first person at the session. Arrive at least five minutes early, so you can welcome persons as they come in. Practice gracious hospitality.

- Greet each person by name when they arrive. This is very important.

- Make sure that your meeting space is comfortable and conducive to group conversation.

- For the best sharing, arrange the chairs in a circle. Directing the group from up front just kills discussion, because it sends the wrong message.

- Begin and end on time. This shows that you honor commitments and respect other people's time.

- Make sure to introduce guests and help them feel welcome.

- If there is business, keep it short.

- When listing to prayer concerns, do not gossip or get sidetracked. You want to build trust in the group and gossip will hinder that.

- Create a climate of openness, encourage individuals to participate in ways that are comfortable for them. Be enthusiastic. **Remember, you set the tone for the class.**

- Some people are uncomfortable talking, so occasionally let them write their responses. If no one answers at first, don't be afraid of a little silence. Count to ten silently; then say something such as, "Would anyone like to go first?" If no one responds, venture an answer yourself. **Have your answers prepared ahead of time**. But don't talk too much. Your answer is only meant to model how to respond, not to dominate the discussion. Then ask for comments and other responses.

- Model openness as you share with the group. Group members will follow your example. If you only share at a surface level, everyone else will follow suit. If you want a richer discussion, you need to share at a deeper level yourself.

- Be aware, however, that it is natural for the conversation to begin at a surface level and then move more deeply as the session goes on. These sessions are designed to begin at a surface level and go progressively deeper.

- Draw out participants without asking them to share what they are unwilling to share. Make eye contact with someone and say something like, "How about someone else?"

- Encourage multiple responses before moving on. If you want more conversation around a response, ask something like, "Has that ever happened to anyone else?"

- If you have trouble getting responses from the group, consider giving your answer first and then just going around the circle. This lowers the anxiety of those who might feel uncomfortable. But indicate that it's ok not to answer.

- Avoid asking "Why?" or "Why do you believe that?" Instead consider asking or giving an example to illustrate the point.

- Affirm responses with comments such as, "Great," or "Thanks," or "I like that," especially if this is the first time someone has spoken during the group session.

- Steer the conversation away from argument. If you feel things heating up, say something like, "You seem to feel strongly about this."

- Give everyone a chance to talk but keep the conversation moving. Moderate to prevent a few individuals from doing all of the talking. Please note that some people will not talk unless you call on them and some will talk all the time if you let them.

- Monitor your own contributions. If you are doing most of the talking, back off.

- Remember that you do not have to have all the answers. Your job is to keep the discussion going and encourage participation. If there are questions that need further research, just write them down and either find an answer or ask someone to find an answer later or consult with a knowledgeable person after the session.

- Consider involving group members in various aspects of the group session, such as asking for volunteers to read Scripture, the closing prayer or say their own, and so forth. Prayers are included in this workbook.

- Before each group session, pray for God's presence, guidance, and power; and throughout the study. Pray weekly or daily for your group members by name and for what God may do in their lives. More than anything else, prayer will encourage and empower you as you lead the group.

- If you really want your small group to be successful, make sure you contact all absentees.

- Don't forget that some people find working on a service project with the group or organizing an event for the group just as meaningful to their spiritual growth as group discussion.

It takes a dedicated leader to make any group go well. Thank you for your commitment. Blessings on your ministry.

Notes

Notes

www.ingramcontent.com/pod-product-compliance
Lightning Source LLC
Chambersburg PA
CBHW082248300426
44110CB00039B/2477